W9-CDL-180

CLOSER LOOK AT

EARTHQUAKES

Joyce Pope

COPPER BEECH BOOKS
Brookfield, Connecticut

© Aladdin Books Ltd 1998
© U.S. text 1998
Designed and produced by
Aladdin Books Ltd
28 Percy Street
London W1P 0LD

*First published in the United States
in 1998 by*
Copper Beech Books,
an imprint of
The Millbrook Press
2 Old New Milford Road
Brookfield, Connecticut 06804

Editor
Alex Edmonds

Designer
Gary Edgar-Hyde

Picture Research
Brooks Krikler Research

Front cover illustration
Gary Edgar-Hyde

Illustrators
Ian Moores
Mike Saunders
Gary Edgar-Hyde

Certain illustrations have appeared in
earlier books created by Aladdin Books.

Printed in Belgium

Library of Congress Cataloging-in-Publication Data
Pope, Joyce.
Earthquakes / Joyce Pope
p. cm. — (Closer look at)
Originally published : London : Franklin Watts, 1996.
Includes index.
Summary: Explains how and why earthquakes happen, their
effect on the environment, and how potential catastrophies could
be prevented by predicting when earthquakes might occur.
ISBN 0-7613-0806-7 (lib. bdg.)
1. Earthquakes—Juvenile literature. [1. Earthquakes.]
I. Title II. Series: Closer look at (Brookfield, Conn.)
QE521.3.P66 1998   97-31924
551.22—dc21   CIP AC

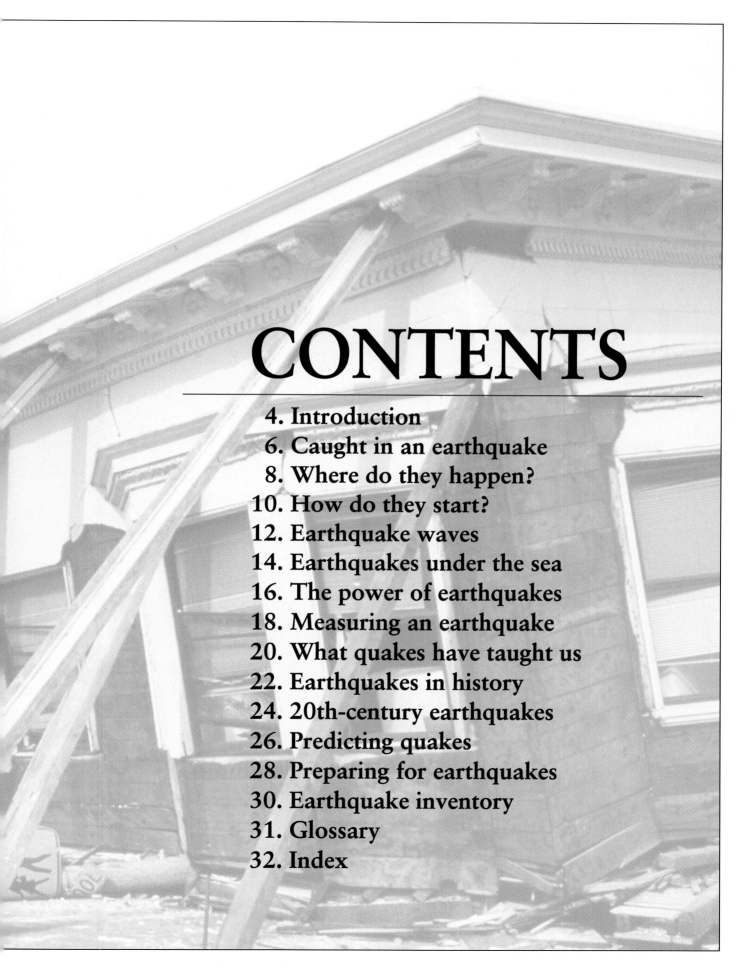

CONTENTS

INTRODUCTION

During an earthquake, the power of the planet shows itself. Rocks deep in the Earth's crust shift and tear, causing devastation to towns and countryside alike. After the quake the change in the surface rocks usually seems slight, but there may well be immense damage to humans and their environment. Over large areas, houses may have been flattened, huge buildings may have fallen, and roads and bridges may be cracked and impassable.

An earthquake strikes without warning. Suddenly, everything that you thought was solid and strong changes. Your house shudders. Run outside and you will see the ground rolling like waves over the sea. As houses and office buildings collapse, power lines may be brought down, and gas mains broken, so fire often adds to the general confusion

CAUGHT IN

The tragedy
These women (above) are survivors of a quake that left 30,000 dead in northern India in 1993. Their homes are flattened and they have lost all they own, and possibly family members. The effect of the quake will be lifelong for them.

THE WORLD TEARS OPEN
In most years there are about 500,000 earthquakes. The majority of these are very small and can only be noticed by very sensitive machines. About 1,000 of them cause some damage, and in most years at least one earthquake is a major catastrophe, such as this earthquake in California (left). Although an earthquake usually starts deep below the ground, it forces the rocks at the surface to form into waves. Most rocks are too fragile for this treatment, so they split apart. Sometimes openings appear and close again. Often, as in this picture (right), surface rocks break and shift, leaving cracks that may be big enough for cars, or even whole houses, to fall into.

ON CLOSER INSPECTION
– The effect

If you are indoors during an earthquake, the room sways like a ship. You can get an idea of what it is like to be in a small earthquake if you stand by a road as a big truck thunders past. The ground shudders, but the moment passes without serious damage.

AN EARTHQUAKE

HOW LONG DO THEY LAST?

Tension in the Earth's crust may build up for hundreds of years, as at the San Andreas Fault in California (below). When it finally reaches breaking point the earthquake takes only a few minutes. Often it lasts for ten seconds or less. If it is big, there may be brief aftershocks.

Earthquakes may happen on land or under the sea. They are rarest in areas of ancient rock that lie at the very center of the continents. They are common at the edges of the great tectonic plates (see p.9) that fit together like a jigsaw over the Earth's surface. The plates push against each other under pressure, and this causes the earthquake.

WHERE DO

The San Andreas Fault

The huge San Andreas Fault system stretches for over 750 miles, following the coast of California. Today it is easy to see the dramatic evidence of the fault in cracked walls and scarred landscapes like the one below.

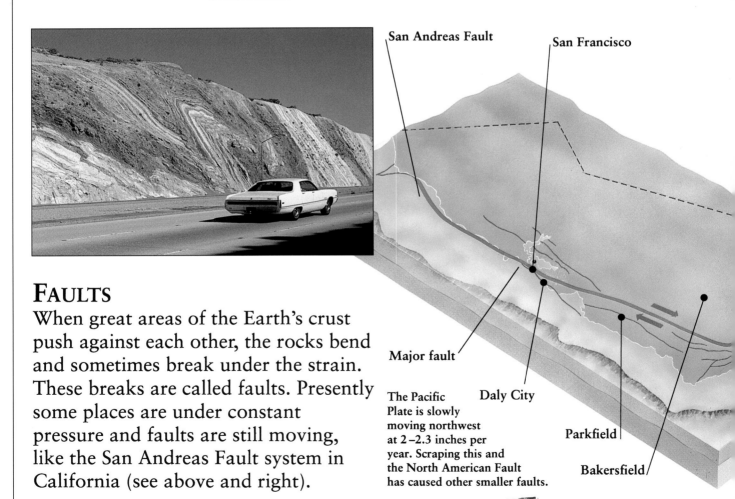

San Andreas Fault

San Francisco

Major fault

Daly City

Parkfield

Bakersfield

FAULTS

When great areas of the Earth's crust push against each other, the rocks bend and sometimes break under the strain. These breaks are called faults. Presently some places are under constant pressure and faults are still moving, like the San Andreas Fault system in California (see above and right).

The Pacific Plate is slowly moving northwest at 2–2.3 inches per year. Scraping this and the North American Fault has caused other smaller faults.

THEY HAPPEN?

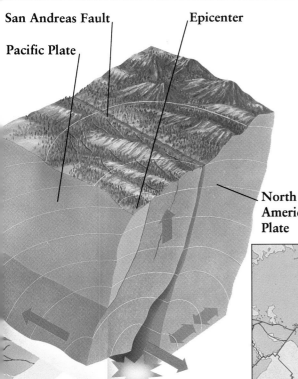

San Andreas Fault Epicenter

Pacific Plate

North American Plate

Focus

This shows the Pacific Plate moving forward and up, after the San Andreas Fault moved under Santa Cruz mountains in 1989.

Los Angeles

THE EARTH'S PLATES

The Earth's surface is not continuous, but is divided into great sections called tectonic plates, which carry the continents and the seabed. There are a number of large plates that are named, and several smaller ones. They move about slowly, shifting at most a few inches a year. Volcanoes and earthquakes occur where plates move against each other.

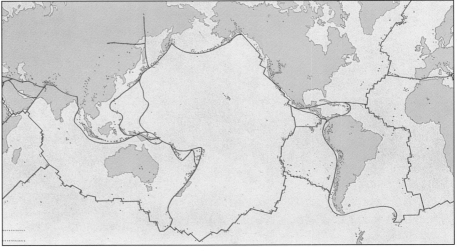

The buildup to the quake

Before the main quake starts, instruments may record a brief tremor. This is called the foreshock. It is caused by the first movement as rocks, stressed to breaking point, begin to fracture. After the main movement, there may be slight adjustments as the rocks finally settle into a new position. These give what are known as aftershocks.

An earthquake starts when rocks in the Earth's crust or mantle tear and slip into a new position. The point at which this happens is called the focus of the earthquake. Waves of energy spread in all directions from the focus. The first point at which they reach the surface is called the epicenter. This is the place where the greatest damage occurs.

HOW DO

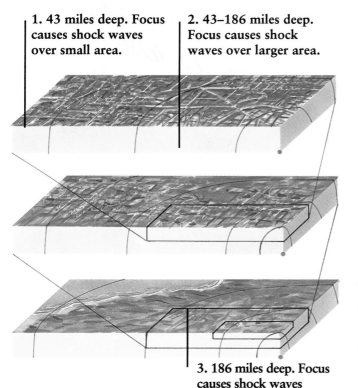

1. 43 miles deep. Focus causes shock waves over small area.

2. 43–186 miles deep. Focus causes shock waves over larger area.

3. 186 miles deep. Focus causes shock waves over huge areas.

This diagram shows how the depth of focus of an earthquake affects how far the shock waves travel, causing damage over a wide area.

THE FOCUS

During an earthquake, in which two plates push into each other, or grind past one another, the focus of the quake is shallow, in the rocks of the crust. Deep-focus earthquakes are caused by one plate riding over the other, pushing it far down into the Earth's mantle. The deeper the focus of an earthquake, the further the waves will pass through the Earth (see left). The focus of the quake can be calculated by finding out how strong the waves are and from which direction they have come.

Oceanic ridge

At an oceanic ridge, hot, molten rock rises and creates strain in the rocks until it is relieved by an earthquake, which will usually be small.

ON CLOSER INSPECTION
– History Unraveled

Old rocks can show us where
earthquakes once took place.
We can see folded rocks that were
squeezed up into folds. Sometimes
they broke and slipped. Geologists
call breaks and slips like this
"faults." The faults in this cliff tell
of ancient stresses and earthquakes.

THEY START?

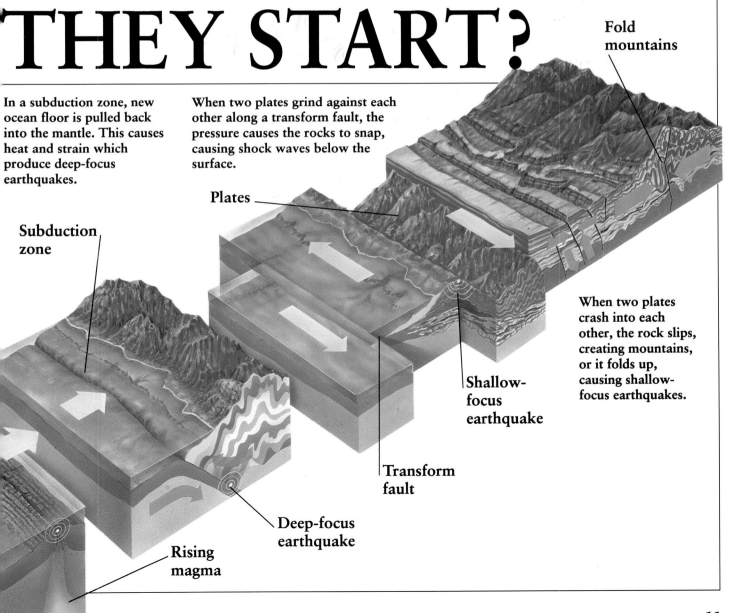

In a subduction zone, new
ocean floor is pulled back
into the mantle. This causes
heat and strain which
produce deep-focus
earthquakes.

When two plates grind against each
other along a transform fault, the
pressure causes the rocks to snap,
causing shock waves below the
surface.

Fold
mountains

Plates

Subduction
zone

When two plates
crash into each
other, the rock slips,
creating mountains,
or it folds up,
causing shallow-
focus earthquakes.

Shallow-
focus
earthquake

Transform
fault

Deep-focus
earthquake

Rising
magma

A slice of the Earth diagram

Plates slide over slush as they move.

Plates and crust.

Lighter, upper mantle

Thicker mantle

Liquid core

Solid core

miles
3,728
3,106
2,485
1,864
1,242
621
0

After foreshocks, the ground is shaken by 3 sets of waves. First come the P (Primary) waves. These travel at about 5 miles per second. They squeeze and pull rocks and liquids as they pass. Then come S (Secondary) waves, which travel at about 4 miles per second. They shake the rocks from side to side.

EARTHQUAKE

Areas where the ground expands

Areas where ground contracts

P-waves are the first to be recorded. They squeeze and stretch the rocks as they pass through the Earth.

A SLICE OF THE EARTH

A wedge cut out of the Earth, like a slice from a cake, would show that it is made of layers of different types of rock (see above). Earthquakes start in the rocks of the crust and the upper part of the mantle.

Length of the wave

S-waves shake the rocks up and down and from side to side. Because S-waves cannot travel through fluids, there are areas of water on the ground where there are no S-waves.

ON CLOSER INSPECTION
– Hidden faults?

The fault, or fracture, that causes these earthquakes is usually deep within the Earth. In some cases it is visible at the surface – for example, at the San Andreas Fault. Faults like this usually produce shallow earthquakes.

WAVES

THE MOST LETHAL WAVES!

The last of the earthquake waves to be felt are called the L-waves. They travel more slowly than others, at not more than about 2.5 miles per second. In spite of this they cause the most damage, for they are only felt on the surface of the Earth.

L-waves make the ground roll beneath your feet. They open chasms in the rocks and shake down buildings.

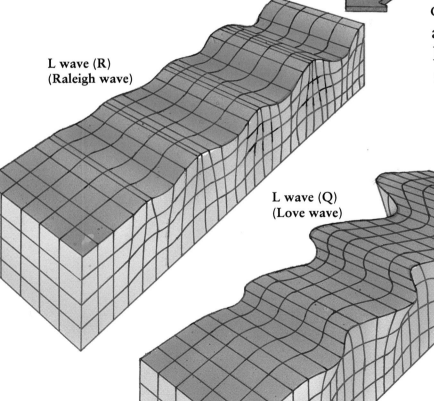

L wave (R)
(Raleigh wave)

L wave (Q)
(Love wave)

Love waves and Raleigh waves (both L-waves) travel over the ground with an up-and-down rolling movement, like ocean waves.

Wet and wild
Tsunamis often cause more damage than the actual earth tremor. They may flood towns and drown thousands of people. One of the biggest this century threw waves 1,738 feet onto the land. Sometimes, as below, the force of the tsunami causes large boats to be stranded far from the sea and general devastation.

Most of the Earth's surface is covered by oceans, and many earthquakes occur under the water. This may be where plates are growing, or where faulting occurs for other reasons. The focus of underwater quakes can be pinpointed, and changes in the seabed can be charted by ships with sensitive depth sounders.

EARTHQUAKES

When the tsunami nears the shore, its waves become closer together, and taller.

The tsunami pounds down on the coast and surges inland. It sweeps away everything in its path.

The word "tsunami" comes from the Japanese, meaning "harbor" and "wave." This picture, painted in about 1820 by Hokusai shows boats about to be overwhelmed by a giant wave, probably a tsunami. Many great earthquake waves have struck Japanese coasts.

UNDER THE SEA

TIDAL WAVE!

Although earthquakes under the sea do not affect the land directly, the sudden change in the seabed can cause tsunamis to be formed. In the open ocean tsunamis are not great – usually not more than 3 feet high. There may be more than 60 miles between one crest and the next. But they travel fast, often at over 400 miles per hour. As a tsunami approaches land where there are beaches and narrow inlets, the water towers into a huge wave, which does tremendous damage when it crashes ashore.

The waves make the sea floor jolt, which creates large sea waves.

When an earthquake occurs below the ocean floor, part of the seabed is forced up.

House problems
Damage caused by earthquakes (above) is often made greater by fires caused by gas or oil leaking. Huge sums of money are needed to repair the damage caused by earthquakes.

The destructive powers of earthquakes are felt most strongly where cities are built on soft rocks such as sands and silts, because L-waves can pass through these most easily. But loss of life and damage to property tend to be greatest where houses and other buildings are made of stone.

THE POWER

1,000 ATOMIC BOMBS

It is difficult to imagine the power of an earthquake. Atomic bombs are the only human inventions that can compare with forces able to move thousands of tons of rocks in a few seconds. Even so, the energy released by a single atomic bomb could cause only a small earthquake. It has been calculated that an earthquake in Mexico City in 1985 was about equal to 1,000 atomic bombs as large as the one that destroyed the city of Hiroshima in 1945.

The force of an earthquake shatters walls and destroys homes (left).

ON CLOSER INSPECTION
– The Bull of Minos

The ancient Greeks believed that a great bull lived in tunnels below the palace of Knossos, in Crete. His bellowing was thought to shake the Earth. This is perhaps how the Greeks explained what happened in an earthquake.

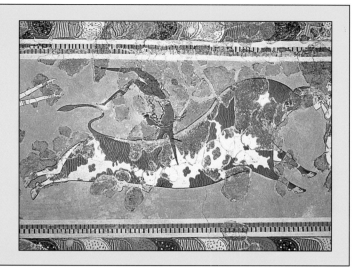

OF EARTHQUAKES

COMMUNICATION PROBLEMS

After an earthquake, rescue can be difficult if entry to the area is hard. The destruction of roads, bridges, and tunnels adds to the chaos caused by earthquakes, as seen left, in the 1995 earthquake at Kobe, Japan. Some bad earthquakes have been in mountainous areas. This has made rescuing victims even harder than usual.

SAN FRANCISCO – 1989

An earthquake may cause damage over a large area. The earthquake in 1989 in San Francisco, California, affected a million square miles of land. In the city damage to buildings and roads was estimated at 6 million dollars (right). Sixty-three people were killed and 4,000 injured.

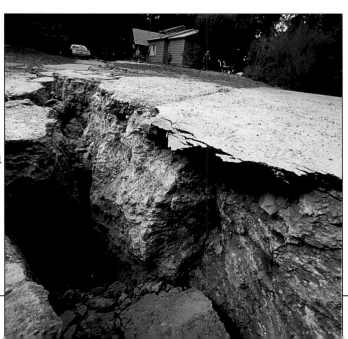

Scientists can tell the strength of a quake using the Richter scale. This is based on the energy released in an earthquake shock, calculated from seismograph readings. The largest Richter number of any recent earthquake was 8.3 (over 7 is considered to be a major earthquake), recorded in the Chilean earthquake of 1960.

MEASURING

Seismographs

A seismograph reading (below) shows the time at which an earthquake takes place, and how long it lasts. The more jagged the line, the greater the shock. The reading from a big quake will show three different periods of shaking, produced by the P-, S-, and L-waves.

MERCALLI SCALE

The Mercalli Scale was first invented in 1902, and modified in 1931, so that it now applies to damage in modern cities. It runs from strength 1, which is a quake felt by very few people, to strength 12, which can totally destroy whole towns and kill all of the inhabitants.

3. Similar to a large passing vehicle.

4. Felt by many people indoors.

1. Felt by only some people.

2. Felt by a few, on upper floors.

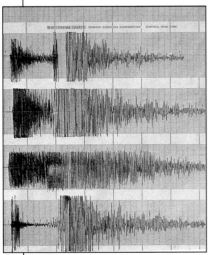

A sensitive spring and a weight are attached to a rigid frame. The frame moves when the ground shakes. A pen records the movement as a line on a rotating drum. Seismographs record vertical and side-to-side movements in the Earth's crust.

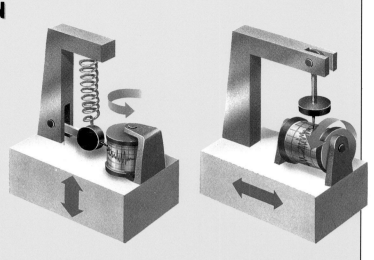

AN EARTHQUAKE

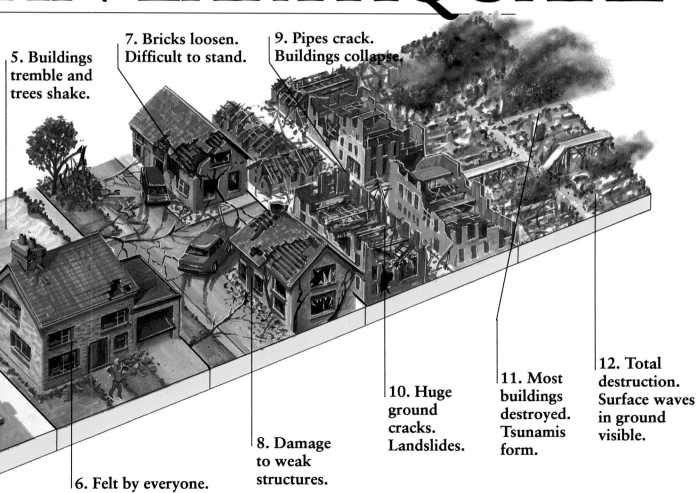

5. Buildings tremble and trees shake.

7. Bricks loosen. Difficult to stand.

9. Pipes crack. Buildings collapse.

6. Felt by everyone. Plaster cracks.

8. Damage to weak structures.

10. Huge ground cracks. Landslides.

11. Most buildings destroyed. Tsunamis form.

12. Total destruction. Surface waves in ground visible.

By measuring the direction and speeds of P- and S-waves, scientists have been able to explore the interior of the Earth. P- and S-waves pass through the mantle at high speeds, but at a depth of about 1,800 miles below the surface, they meet the Earth's outer core and the S-waves can go no further.

Earthquake zone

At a depth of about 21 miles from the surface of an earthquake zone (above), the speed of P- and S-waves changes. Geologists have tried to drill down to reach this point, where the interior of the Earth really begins.

S-WAVES

The S-waves stop, because the Earth's outer core is made of melted rocks. The side-to-side S-waves cannot pass through liquids. P-waves can. They also pass through the solid core, but the waves change direction slightly when they reach the liquid outer core. They emerge into the mantle and the plates on the surface of the far side of the world.

WHAT QUAKES

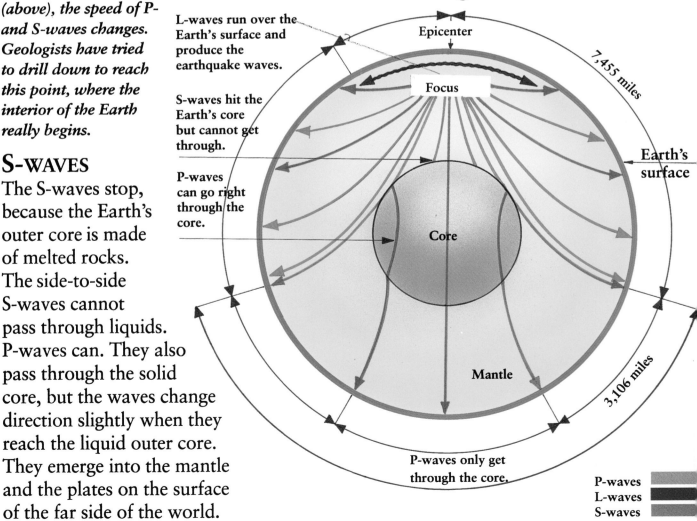

L-waves run over the Earth's surface and produce the earthquake waves.

S-waves hit the Earth's core but cannot get through.

P-waves can go right through the core.

Epicenter

Focus

7,455 miles

Earth's surface

Core

Mantle

3,106 miles

P-waves only get through the core.

P-waves
L-waves
S-waves

ON CLOSER INSPECTION
– Explosive work

Geologists may need to explore
and map the rocks below the
Earth's surface. They often mimic
earthquakes by making explosions
below ground. This work tells
geologists where rocks bearing
oil or minerals occur.

HAVE TAUGHT US

MAN-MADE EARTHQUAKES

Human beings can cause earthquakes
too. Often they are produced when
a dam has been built, such as the
Hoover Dam (below), holding up
millions of tons of incredibly
heavy water. The rocks below the
dam have been stressed and shifted,
like those at the edges of plates.
This tension then results
in earthquakes.

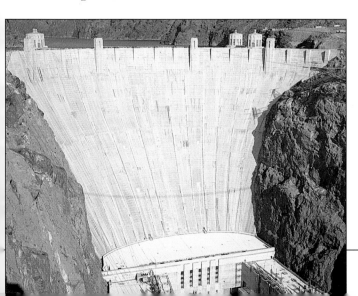

DAM DISASTERS

The Kariba Dam in Africa (above) holds
back the world's largest artificial lake. It
is a major project which disrupts rocks
below the Earth's surface. Another
example is the Hoover Dam in Arizona.
In the years after it had been built, 6,000
minor earthquakes were recorded.

Port Royal

In 1692 a great earthquake destroyed Port Royal in Jamaica (below). Twenty thousand people were killed in the earthquake. Port Royal was an important pirate center for the West Indies, and had traded in slaves and rum. Because of this, many people believed that the earthquake was God's way of punishing the town.

In many parts of the world, throughout all human history, earthquakes have brought terror to city dwellers. Ephesus and many other beautiful ancient cities of what is now southern Turkey, have been wrecked by earthquakes. Even remains in South America, of Mayan and Inca civilizations, show earthquake damage as far back as the 4th century B.C.

EARTHQUAKES

LISBON EARTHQUAKE

In Portugal, in November 1755, shock waves from the first tremors of what was to be a devastating earthquake traveled from the epicenter to the city of Lisbon in seconds. As the earthquake shook the city, people rushed into the open, but many were killed by collapsing buildings. Fire followed, then huge tsunamis raced in from the ocean and swept across all but the highest part of the town. About 60,000 people were killed in Lisbon, and others died in nearby Spain and North Africa.

On Closer Inspection
– Chinese quake sensor

A tremor causes a weight inside a pot to swing. This causes one of the dragons on the outside of the pot to open its mouth and drop a bronze ball. Metal frogs with open mouths surround the pot to catch the falling balls. The frog that is the farthest away from the epicenter catches the ball first.

IN HISTORY

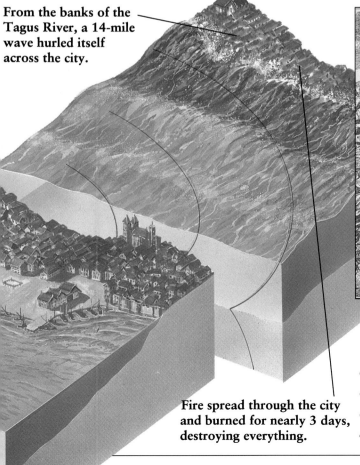

From the banks of the Tagus River, a 14-mile wave hurled itself across the city.

Fire spread through the city and burned for nearly 3 days, destroying everything.

LISABONA

Lisbon ruins

This woodcut depicts the general devastation caused by the 1755 earthquake. It shows the effects of the tsunamis which not only destroyed homes and towns but also tore apart ships and boats on the ocean.

Present-day earthquakes are part of the final phases of the formation of great mountains such as the Himalayas. Although this began millions of years ago, earthquakes still continue as the plates that carry the continents push into each other.

20th-CENTURY

CALIFORNIAN EARTHQUAKES

In 1906 an earthquake measuring about 7.8 on the Richter scale struck San Francisco, killing over 700 people. In 1989 another, measuring 7.1, caused huge damage when a concrete highway collapsed. Los Angeles has also suffered from powerful quakes. The San Andreas and other faults run near to both cities.

Turkey

Turkey (above) and the countries of western Asia have been the site of many great earthquakes in the past. This is because the Turkish Plate is being pushed by two other plates, like the blades of a pair of scissors. By looking at the history of the quakes, scientists have learned how the plate is moving.

Scientists use modern camera techniques to construct how it would appear if you were in a serious earthquake (right).

When an earthquake strikes, homeless people need shelter, blankets, and food. Trained sniffer dogs are sometimes sent to detect survivors buried under rubble.

EARTHQUAKES

INDIA

Northern India (below), Pakistan, and Afghanistan have all suffered in recent years from earthquakes registering between 6.8 and 7.0 on the Richter scale. Because these quakes have taken place in remote regions, few people have been killed.

JAPAN

The crowded cities of Japan have suffered more from earthquakes than any other part of the world. The most recent serious quake was in 1995 (above), when a quake killed over 5,000 people and injured over 25,000 in Kobe. This was caused by a fault that had not shifted for 1,000 years and was thought to be safe.

The race is on
Scientists in Japan (above) study computers for signs of earthquake activity. Laser beams can also be reflected across fault lines to show tiny ground movements. The beams are sent from specially made huts (right).

To predict an earthquake, scientists need to discover where and how fast rocks are moving along geological faults. Seismologists have discovered several warning signs in the buildup of an earthquake – such as changes in seismic waves and lots of minor tremors along plate edges. Using modern technology along with these signals, they try and predict earthquakes.

PREDICTING

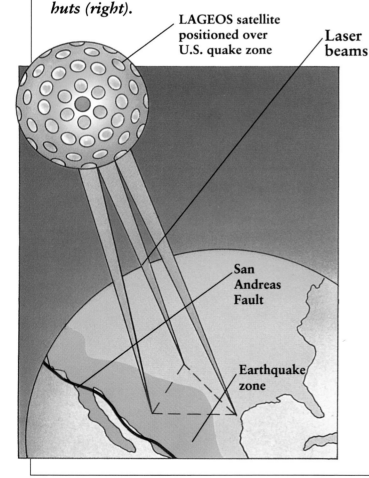

LAGEOS satellite positioned over U.S. quake zone

Laser beams

San Andreas Fault

Earthquake zone

BE PREPARED
In California they expect an earthquake measuring 6.7 on the Richter scale every 11 years. But during the last 195 years there have been far fewer than this, so it looks as if the rocks sliding past each other in the faults are stuck. Scientists say they will soon move, causing an earthquake – but they don't know when.

ON CLOSER INSPECTION
– Animal problems

In parts of the world without scientific equipment, people watch animal behavior to give them a clue about earthquakes that are on the way. Many animals, such as horses, show signs of distress. They are probably reacting to small foreshocks that humans cannot feel.

EARTHQUAKES

STRAIN METER

The white, trash can-like object protects a hole containing a strain meter (below). This records the amount of water underground and in the rocks, which changes with the pressure of seismic movements on the rocks. Solar panels power the equipment.

CREEP METER

A creep meter (above) measures rock movements along a fault. If water is pumped into moving fault areas it acts as a lubricant. The rocks move smoothly against each other and so cause only small ground tremors.

People living in earthquake zones have to be prepared for the worst. Tokyo, Japan, one of the most quake struck cities in the world, monitors fault movements constantly to warn of large quakes. There are trained disaster teams ready to go to work in an emergency, and food and blankets and huge supplies of water for fighting fires are held in readiness.

PREPARING

BEING PREPARED

The Transamerica building in San Francisco (left) stands 836 feet high. It is built to withstand even the most severe earthquake. Its triangular frame is supported by concrete-covered steel columns to give it the necessary strength.

Schoolchildren in Japan practice their earthquake drills (right).

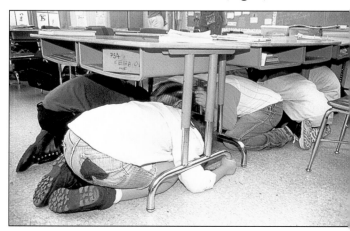

ON CLOSER INSPECTION
– Street safety

Simple precautions can help reduce earthquake damage. Wide, straight streets, like these in San Francisco, can help to prevent the spread of fire. Wide streets also leave space between the rubble of fallen buildings for the emergency services to rescue people.

FOR EARTHQUAKES

Chimneys are secured with special brackets.

Beams and joists are reinforced.

A SAFE HOME

There are now ways to make houses safer. They should be low, with strengthened foundations and upper walls, and beams firmly fixed to withstand the swaying L-waves that cause most of the damage. Some of the more bizarre-looking designs include this San Franciscan home (above).

Foundations are reinforced with steel rods. Walls are secured to the foundations.

Water heaters, boilers etc. are secured to prevent them from breaking loose and cracking gas pipes.

A fault in the ground in San Francisco, California.

EARTHQUAKE INVENTORY

Year	Place	Richter Scale No.	Number of casualties
1201	Eastern Mediterranean		1.1 million dead
1692	Port Royal, Jamaica		more than 2,000 dead
1755	Lisbon, Portugal		more than 160,000 dead
1873	Southern Italy		51,000 dead
1906	Colombia/Ecuador	8.6	
1906	Valparaiso, Chile	8.6	20,000 dead
1906	San Francisco, CA	8.3	503 dead

Cleaning up after the 1991 quake in Georgia.

Year	Place	Richter Scale No.	Number of casualties
1911	Sinkiang, China	–	
1920	Gansu, China	–	
1923	Sagami Bay, Tokyo	8.2	
1933	Japanese Trench	8.5	
1955	North Assam, India	8.6	
1960	Chile	8.9	
1964	Alaska	8.4	131 killed, more than $750 million damage
1976	Tangshan, China	8.2	242,000 dead
1985	Mexico City, Mexico	8.1	
1988	Armenia	6.9	25,000 dead

The aftermath of the 1991 quake in northern India.

Year	Place	Richter Scale No.	Number of casualties
1989	San Francisco, CA	7.1	62 dead
1990	Iran	7.7	40,000 dead
1990	Peru	6.3	more than 100 dead
1990	Romania	6.5-7.0	about 70 dead
1990	Philippines	7.7	over 1,500 dead
1991	Northern India	7.1	500 dead
1991	Hindu Kush, Afghanistan	6.8	1,200 dead
1991	Central America	7.5	more than 80 dead
1991	Georgia,	7.2	more than 100 dead
1995	Kobe, Japan	7.2	5,502 dead

Aftershocks Vibrations caused by the movement of rocks as they settle into their new position after an earthquake.

Crust The outermost layer of the Earth, consisting of rocks that form the land and ocean floor.

Epicenter The point on the Earth's surface immediately above the focus of an earthquake.

Fault A crack in the rocks that form the Earth's surface. Blocks of rock separated by faults may move vertically or sideways.

Focus The point where the rocks start pushing or grinding against one another, producing an earthquake.

Fold A bend in layers of rock caused by plate movements.

Lava Molten rock that pours from a volcano.

Magma Molten rock that lies below the Earth's crust in the mantle.

Mantle The layer of the Earth between the crust and the outer core.

Oceanic ridges These occur down the middle of the major oceans where the crustal plates are moving apart. Molten rock from beneath the crust constantly wells up between the two plates. The ridges are formed from the cooling lava creating new ocean floor.

Richter scale A scale measuring the strength of an earthquake by using information from a seismograph.

Seismograph An instrument for measuring the time, size, and direction of an earthquake.

Seismologist A scientist who studies earthquakes.

Subduction zone A place where the ocean floor is submerging into the mantle beneath another plate. The heat from the mantle causes the rock to melt.

GLOSSARY

Tectonic plate One of the large slabs of rock that form the Earth's crust. The plates move very slowly as they float on the molten magma beneath them. Continental plates are five or six times thicker than oceanic plates.

Tremor Also called a foreshock, this is a vibration of the ground caused by the first movement as stressed rocks begin to break.

Tsunami A large tidal wave caused by an earthquake or volcanic eruption, which often does tremendous damage to coastal regions.

Volcano A rift or vent in the Earth's crust through which molten rock erupts from deep within the Earth and flows over the surface.

INDEX

Photo credits

Smoky Mountain Rose

An Appalachian Cinderella

by
ALAN SCHROEDER

pictures by
BRAD SNEED

Dial Books for Young Readers / New York

For Bob San Souci, a terrific storyteller and a good friend
—A.S.

For Emily
—B.S.

Published by Dial Books for Young Readers
A Division of Penguin Books USA Inc.
375 Hudson Street
New York, New York 10014

Designed by Nancy R. Leo
Printed in Hong Kong
First Edition
7 9 10 8 6

Library of Congress Cataloging in Publication Data
Schroeder, Alan.
Smoky Mountain Rose : an Appalachian Cinderella /
by Alan Schroeder ; pictures by Brad Sneed.
p.   cm.
Based on Charles Perrault's Cendrillon.
Summary: In this variation on the Cinderella story, based on the Charles Perrault
version but set in the Smoky Mountains, Rose loses her glass slipper at
a party given by the rich feller on the other side of the creek.
ISBN 0-8037-1733-4. — ISBN 0-8037-1734-2 (lib. bdg.)
[1. Fairy tales. 2. Folklore—France.] I. Sneed, Brad, ill.
II. Perrault, Charles, 1628–1703. Cendrillon. III. Cinderella. English. IV. Title.
PZ8.S3125Sm 1997   398.21'09768'89—dc20   [E]   92-1250   CIP   AC

The artwork was prepared with watercolor.

❦❦ Author's Note ❦❦

The story of *Cinderella* is one of the most popular and well-known of all fairy tales. It is also one of the oldest: Its roots can be traced back to China, circa 850 A.D. For Western readers, the most familiar retelling of *Cinderella* is Charles Perrault's "Cendrillon," which was published in Paris in 1697. It is upon this version that I have based my own story, *Smoky Mountain Rose.*

American versions of the tale abound. "Catskins," "Ashpet," and "Rush Cape" (or "Cap o' Rushes") are all dialect retellings (the latter mingles the stories of *Cinderella* and *King Lear*). In "Ashpet," the heroine is not part of the family, but a "hired girl," and her great dream is to go to the church meeting, not the palace ball. The fairy godmother is a peculiar old witch-woman, and near the end of the story the wicked sisters take Ashpet to "the swimmin' place," where she is caught by the "Old Hairy Man" who inhabits the lake.

"Catskins" is unique, not for its use of dialect, but for its unsympathetic heroine. At no point does Catskins seem to be a victim; she comes across as self-centered, untrustworthy, and materialistic. The stepsister, on the other hand, is presented as kindly and generous, even lending Catskins a dress for the "big dance at the King's house."

"Ashpet" and "Catskins" can be found in Richard Chase's delightful *Grandfather Tales* (Houghton Mifflin, 1948). "Rush Cape" appears in Chase's *American Folk Tales and Songs* (New American Library of World Literature, 1956). Finally, an interesting overview of *Cinderella* can be found in *The Classic Fairy Tales* by Iona and Peter Opie (Oxford University Press, 1974).

Now lis'en.

Smack in the heart o' the Smoky Mountains, there was this old trapper livin' in a log cabin with his daughter. One night, while Rose was fryin' a mess o' fish, the trapper, he starts lookin' dejected-like.

"I reckon it's hard on ye, not havin' a ma," he said. "Tell me, Rose, would ye lak me to git hitched again? There's a widow woman with two daughters down the road a piece. Way I see it, we'd all fit together neater'n a jigsaw."

"I don't mind," said Rose, settin' a plate o' corn bread on the table. "You go a-courtin', Pa, if you think it's best."

So before the huckleberries was fit for pickin', the trapper got himself hitched for the second time. That's when the trouble started a-brewin'.

Ye see, Gertie, the new wife, she was just about the crossest, fearsomest woman that side o' Tarbelly Creek. And her two daughters—why, they were so mean they'd steal flies from a blind spider. And vain? Them girls could waste a whole day admirin' themselves in the mirror.

"Ain't I purty?" Annie would say, peering into the glass.

"Not as purty as me!" Liza Jane would retort. "Y'all watch, someday I'm gonna marry me a fine gentleman—go to Memphis and live lak a lady!"

Rose, on the other hand, was a sweet li'l thing, always lookin' out for others and takin' care of sick critters, and the like. Annie and Liza Jane couldn't stand the sight of her. To be orn'ry, they dressed her in the sorriest-lookin' rags and made her do plumb near every chore.

Well, it just about broke the trapper's heart to see his daughter out milkin' the cow and collectin' the firewood and churnin' the butter. He woulda talked to Gertie 'bout it, but talkin' to her was like kickin' an agitated rattler. The trapper figgered it was best to say nothin' at all.

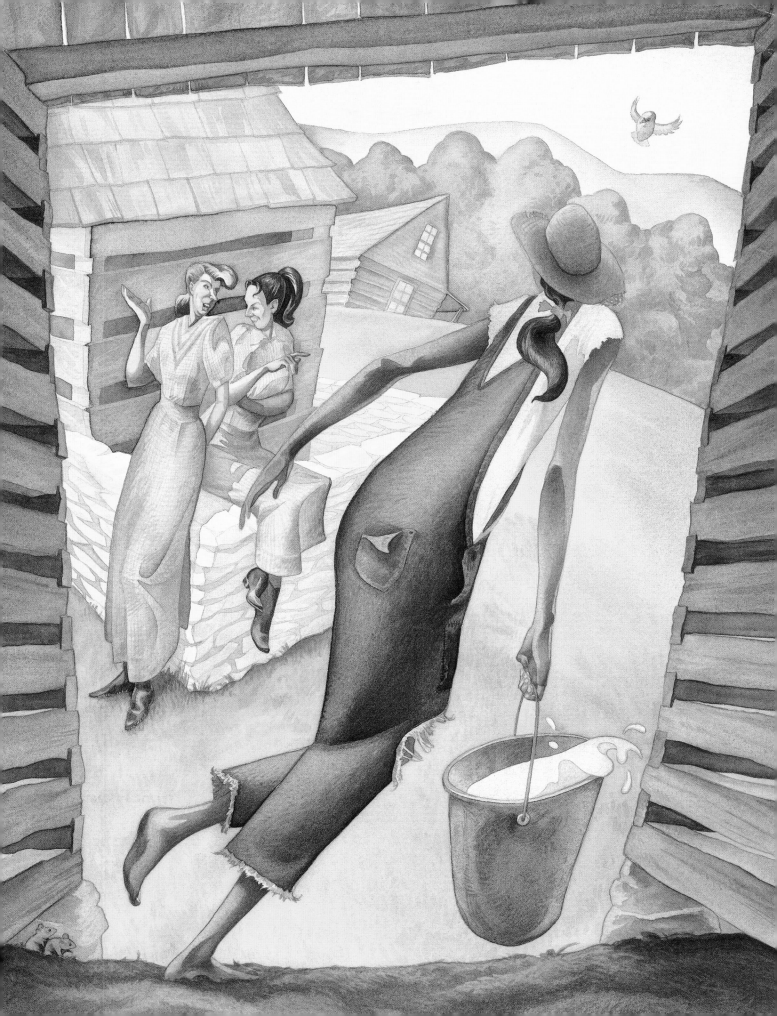

This went on for a long time. Then one day the trapper up and died. Rose had loved her pa somethin' fierce, and for days on end she couldn't stop a-weepin'.

Finally Gertie lit into her, mean as a hornet. "Shet up that cryin'," she screeched, "or I'm gonna feed ye t' the dogs, ye hear?"

From then on, Rose's life was just about as hard as it could be. Chores from sunup t' sundown. Course, she thought of runnin' away, but she didn't have anywhere to go. She figgered she just had to set it out and wait for a better day to come 'long.

Now it so happens that on the other side o' the creek, there was this real rich feller—made his fortune in sowbellies and grits. Well, this feller wasn't hitched yet, so one day he gets the bright idea to invite all the neighbor-people to a fancy ol' party, thinkin' he might find himself a wife. When Annie and Liza Jane got their invitation, they plumb near went crazy with excitement.

"I'm gonna order me a brand-new dress out of that there catalog!" Annie declared.

"No, you ain't!" cried Liza Jane. "That cat'log is mine, you skunk! Take your hands off it!"

Now Rose, she sorta figgered she was invited too. When Annie and Liza Jane heard that, they started a-howlin': "Lawd-a-marcy! Who'd want to dance with a dirt clod lak you?"

For the next few days they worked Rose like they was fixin' to kill her. A full hour before the sun was up, she'd be ironin' their dresses and polishin' their shoes and every other durn fool thing. Now Rose, she wanted to go to the party somethin' awful, but she held her tongue for fear of bein' laughed at again.

The actual night of the shindig the two sisters were downright hateful.

"Hand me that comb, stupid!"

"Tie up my hair ribbon!"

"Whar's my corset?"

Rose ran left and right, tryin' to keep up with their demands. Finally, toward seven o'clock, Gertie and her daughters piled into the tater wagon. Whippin' the mule, they went a-rumblin' down the dirt road, chortlin' out "Skip t' M' Lou" at the top of their lungs.

Rose, meanwhile, sat next to the pigsty and cried. Far off 'cross the creek she could hear the sound of fiddle music. That made her cry even harder.

Just then one of the hogs comes moseyin' up to the fence and starts talkin' to her.

"Ye shore look mis'rable, honey. But don't ye fret none. I know magic and I kin help."

Rose, she just stared, figgerin' she'd done lost her wits. But the hog kept right on talkin'.

"First of all, we gotta get ye out o' them rags. Now stand up and turn around real fast, like ye got a whompus cat bitin' at yer britches."

Rose did just what the hog told her. When she looked down, she was wearin' the purtiest party dress she ever laid eyes on.

"I must be dreamin'," she said to herself.

The hog studied her real careful-like. "Lookin' good, sister—but time's a-wastin'. We gotta get ye over to that shindig. Go fetch me a mushmelon and two field mice."

Again, Rose did just what she was told.

"Now watch," said the hog, and directly the mushmelon was turned into a big ol' wagon. And the mice? Two strong horses, with silky manes and shiny teeth—real show critters.

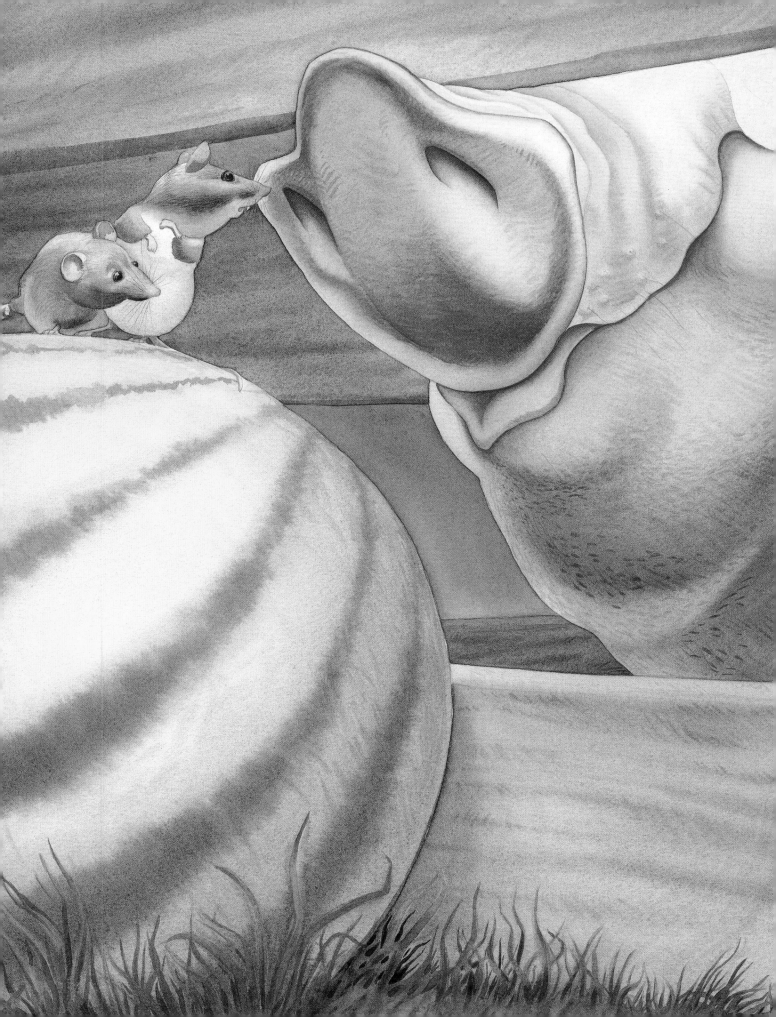

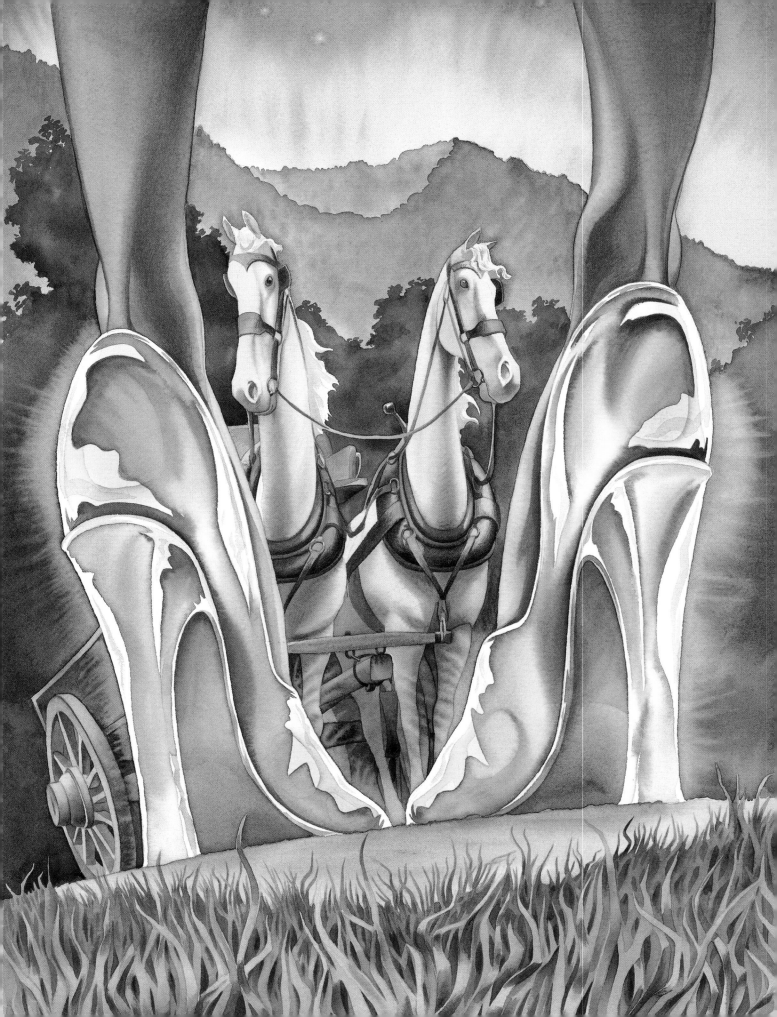

Rose was thrilled t' pieces. She was all set to hop up on the wagon, when the hog let out a big snort. "Why, look at them filthy bare feet! That won't do t'all. Close your eyes. . . . Now open 'em."

Rose looked down. On each foot, she was wearin' a sparklin' glass slipper.

"Ye like 'em?" asked the hog.

"Well," said Rose, tryin' to be polite, "they're not too pract'cal for square dancin', but they sure are purty."

The hog watched as Rose climbed up into the wagon.

"Now don't forget: The spell's only good till midnight, so ye gotta be home by then."

"I'll remember," said Rose, and off she went, a-rumblin' down the dirt road, just as happy as can be.

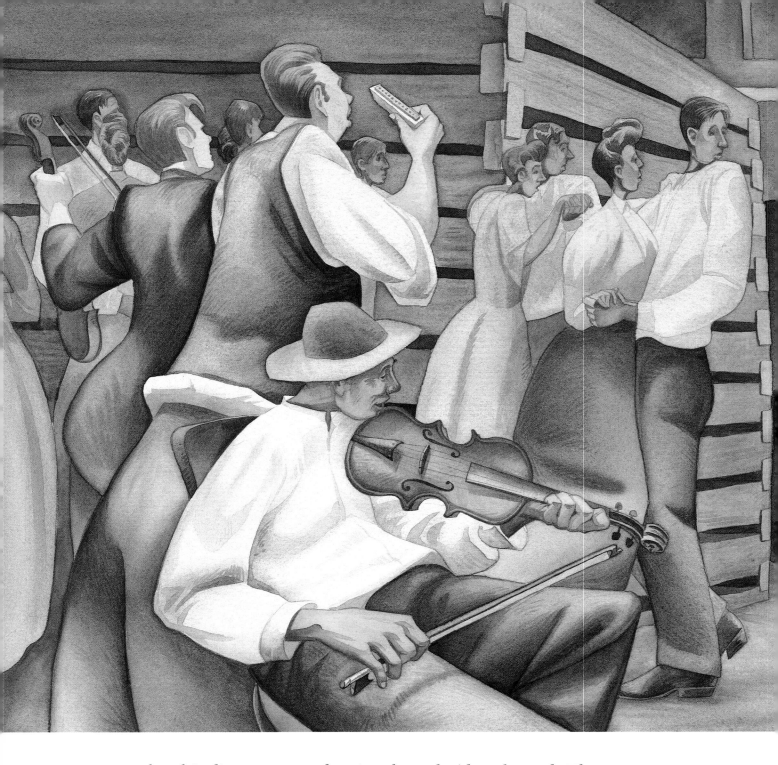

The shindig was even fancier than she'd reckoned. There were two fiddlers, a harmonica man, even a square-dance caller come all the way from Nashville. Everyone was dancin' and laughin' and drinkin' cup after cup o' sarsaparilla.

Now the rich feller, he wasn't havin' such a good time. No one had caught his fancy, see—and then, all of a sudden Rose came in through

the big barn door. She looked so purty that everyone stopped dead in their tracks. The two stepsisters, they pract'cally choked on their cider. "Well, shet my mouth!" one of 'em whispered. "How'd *she* get in here, and whar'd she git all them clothes?"

"I oughta wring her neck!" snapped the other. "She's been goin' through my bood-whar!"

They watched, jaws a-droppin', as the rich feller went hurryin' up to Rose, thrustin' out his hand. "Pleased to meet ye, missy," he said, real friendly. "My name's Seb. How 'bout takin' a turn round the dance floor?"

"My pleasure," said Rose, and off they went, arm in arm.

Neighbors cleared a space and watched as the two lovebirds started promenadin' to the tune o' "Baldy Holler."

> *"Eight hands up and go to the left,*
> *Backwards now, and home ye go!"*

All evenin' long, Rose and Seb kicked up their heels, havin' a high ol' time. Gertie and her two daughters stood off to the side, madder'n blazes. "Look at her," sneered Gertie, "sashayin' round lak she's the belly o' the ball. I'll fix her when she gits home—give her a list o' chores she won't never finish."

Just then Rose happened to glance at the big granddaddy clock in the corner.

"Tarnation!" she cried. "It's midnight!"

Without another word, she went dashin' out the barn door. Poor thing was runnin' so fast, one of her glass slippers went flyin' off into the dirt. She'd a-fetched it, but there warn't time.

"Come back!" cried Seb, chasin' after her. But Rose's wagon was already rattlin' down the road just as fast as it could go.

No sooner was she out o' sight than everythin' turned back the way it used t' be. The wagon was a mushmelon again, and Rose had to walk home dressed in rags. Only thing that hadn't changed was the remainin' glass slipper, which she tucked in her pocket for safe-keepin'.

Before goin' indoors, Rose stopped at the sty to say thank you.

"Anytime, sugar," said the hog.

Now Gertie and her daughters, they came tearin' home 'bout ten minutes later. Rose was already asleep by the fire.

"Ain't ye gonna whip her now, Ma?" said Liza Jane.

"My whippin' arm's tired. I'll do it tomorrow," said Gertie. "You gals git to bed now and git yer beauty sleep. Don't you worry—there'll be fireworks in the mornin'."

Sure enough, the next day Gertie lit into Rose somethin' awful. "Showin' up at that party, makin' my girls look lak fools!" she screeched. "I'll larn ye!" Grabbin' the switch, she was all set to whip Rose, when her two daughters came flyin' up the hill.

"Listen, Ma!" cried Annie. "That rich feller, he found Rose's shoe in the dirt, and now he's goin' round t' every house to find the owner!"

"And that ain't all!" said Liza Jane. "That feller, Ma, he's plumb crazy—says he's gettin' hitched with the first person it fits on, and I reckon it's gonna be me!"

"Well, then, harry up and git ready," said Gertie. "And listen, y'all, whichever of you gets the weddin' ring and moves to Memphis, I'm comin' along—ye ain't leavin' me behind!" Then, turnin' to Rose, Gertie warned: "You stay outta sight, or I'll blister yer rump somethin' fierce."

Half an hour later Seb came rattlin' up the road in his wagon. Gertie was there a-waitin' on the porch, shuckin' peas.

"Why, it's the sowbelly and grits feller," she said, actin' real surprised. "Come on in and set a spell. Understand ye found my daughter's shoe."

Before Seb had even said "Howdy-do," Annie came flyin' out on the porch, stickin' out her foot. "Me first!" she yelled, settin' herself down on a big milk bucket. Now Seb, he commences to tuggin' and pullin', but gettin' the slipper onto her big foot was like tryin' to stretch a li'l bitty sausage skin over a side o' beef.

"Git out o' my way," said Liza Jane, pushin' her sister aside. And right away she starts a-battin' her eyes at Seb. "I wanna thank ye for returnin' my shoe," she said. "I 'bout fell into a fidget o' fear when I saw it was gone." But Seb could tell she was just sweet-talkin'. The minute the tuggin' started, Liza Jane purt-near went blue in the face. "Lemme git the axe," she said, a-gaspin'. "I'll get that shoe on if it kills me!"

Just then Seb spotted Rose standin' off near the pigsty. "Warn't you at the shindig last night?" he called out.

Rose went on feedin' the hogs lak she didn't hear him.

"Come over here, and stick out yer foot," Seb told her. He watched as Rose came a-walkin' toward him. "You look mighty familiar, missy. Come on now, just set yerself down on this here bucket and stick out yer tootsie."

Annie and Liza Jane held their breath as Rose stretched out her pretty li'l foot. "Now hold still," Seb told her, and wouldn't ye know it, the slipper went glidin' right on, just as smooth as butter!

When Gertie saw that, she started a-screechin': "That weasel, she's a-trickin' ye! Why, my daughters are a heap purtier'n her!"

But Seb, he didn't pay her no mind—happy as a pig in a peanut patch, he took up Rose's hand and held it tight.

"I knew I'd find ye!" he whispered, and Rose nodded, all teary-eyed. Then, rememberin' the other slipper, she took it out of her pocket and put it on. Very same moment, the hog started snortin' and kickin' up a fuss, and when Rose looked down again, she was wearin' the exact same dress she had on at the shindig—lookin' just as purty as bluebonnets in spring.

'Pon seein' that, the two stepsisters, they done burst into tears. "Our precious li'l sister gonna be marryin' into money!" And they set to fussin' over her lak they jest loved her to pieces. Now Rose, she could have turned her back on 'em, but she didn't. Sweet thing, she figgered it was best t' fergive and forget.

"I love ye like soup loves salt," she told 'em, and from then on Annie and Liza Jane never gave 'er a moment o' grief or heartache.

And the weddin' that followed? Well, it was jest 'bout the biggest shindig ever seen in the Smoky Mountains. To this day, Rose and Seb are still livin' there, and folks reckon they're 'bout the happiest two-some in all o' Tarbelly Creek.